Henry Martyn Dexter

Pilgrim Memoranda

Henry Martyn Dexter

Pilgrim Memoranda

ISBN/EAN: 9783337294144

Printed in Europe, USA, Canada, Australia, Japan

Cover: Foto ©Lupo / pixelio.de

More available books at **www.hansebooks.com**

Pilgrim Memoranda.

By Henry Martyn Dexter.

TODD, PRINTER, Boston.

1870.

CHRONOLOGICAL GLANCE

AT PROMINENT FACTS OF INTEREST,

IN CONNECTION WITH THE

Pilgrim Fathers, and their History.

1380. Wycliffe completed his translation of the Bible, multiplied copies by the aid of transcribers ; and, by God's blessing on His Word, thus unbound from the fetters of alien tongues, a spirit of inquiry was generated, and the seeds sown of that religious revolution, which a little more than a century later, astonished and overturned the world.

1418. Council of Constance ordered Wycliffe's bones to be ungraved and burned for those of a heretic.

1534. Henry the Eighth of England, for the reason that the Pope would not divorce him from Katharine, his wife, divorced the Church of England from its allegiance to Rome.

1550. Puritanism dates from John Hooper's "scrupling the vestments," and refusing to take the oath of supremacy, until King Edward had run his pen through a part of it.

1554. The Frankfort congregation of exiles arose, under the persecuting reign of "Bloody Mary," and the Puritan separation began with Englishmen outside of England.

1566. Date of separation in England, by Puritans who were shut out of the Church, and restrained of the press, and who thought, as separate congregations had for some time been existing at Frankfort, Geneva, and even in London, it might be right, and their duty, to come out and be separate from the corruptions and superstitions swaying the English Church, and its service.

1570. Thomas Cartwright pushed the fundamental proposition to reduce all things in reforming the Church to the apostolical way, as contained in the New Testament. For this he was expelled from Oxford, and took refuge abroad. Coming back seven years after, he maintained that government by the eldership is of divine appointment and obligation — anticipating, mainly, the views and practices of the Presbyterian party of the time of the Commonwealth.

1582. ROBERT BROWNE threw a new element into the conflict of opinion which was agitating the English people (under Elizabeth), by evolving from the New Testament, essentially, the Democratic system of Church polity.

1591. A church of English exiles, actuated by the principles of Browne, but misliking his name, was formed at Amsterdam, of which Henry Ainsworth became pastor.

1593. Henry Barrow, John Greenwood and John Penry put to death for their Congregational principles.

1606. The Mayflower Church was formed by mutual covenant, at Scrooby in Nottinghamshire.

1607. Harried out of England, this Church begins to fly to Holland, and in the next spring, all get over to Amsterdam, where they continue about a year.

1608. The Mayflower Church removed to Leyden, where Robinson was sole pastor, and William Brewster was chosen elder.

1611. $\frac{25\ April.}{5\ May.}$ John Robinson and others of his church bought a house in the Kloksteeg in Leyden, near the University, which "being large," was both occupied by him, and used by them as their place of Sabbath worship.

1615. $\frac{26\ Aug.}{5\ Sept.}$ Robinson became matriculated in the University. Age, thirty-nine.

1620. $\frac{1}{11}$ July. The last revised conditions of the agreement of the English merchants with the intending colonists were settled, and the emigration to America finally and absolutely determined on.

1620. More particular schedule of the events of their emigration hither, and of the first six months of their settlement — in illustration of their sufferings in laying the foundations of civil and religious liberty here.

Day.	Old Style.	New Style.	
Tues.	11 July.	21 July.	Left Leyden.
Sat.	5 Aug.	15 Aug.	Sailed from Southampton, (two ships.)
Sab.	13 "	23 "	Put back to Dartmouth.
Wed.	23 "	2 Sept.	Sailed again.
——	———	——	Put back the second time to Plymouth, and Speedwell dismissed.
Wed.	6 Sept.	16 "	Sailed from Plymouth, (102 in the Mayflower.)
Mon.	6 Nov.	16 Nov.	William Butten dies at sea.
Thurs.	9 "	19 "	Saw Cape Cod.
Sat.	11 "	21 "	Anchored in Provincetown harbor, signed the compact, chose Carver Governor, and went ashore.
Mon.	13 "	23 "	Unshipped the shallop, and went ashore to wash.
Wed.	15 "	25 "	Started on first expedition inland.
Thurs.	16 "	26 "	Found springs in Truro, went as far as Pamet River, found a kettle, dug up corn, etc.
Fri.	17 "	27 "	Sunk the kettle in the pond, and went back to ship.
Mon.	27 "	7 Dec.	Second and larger exploring party started in shallop and get to East Harbor Creek.
Tues.	28 "	8 "	Went on to Pamet River, and inland from it.
Wed.	29 "	9 "	Revisited Cornhill, and Master Jones and a part went back to the ship.
Thurs.	30 "	10 "	Found wigwams, graves, etc., and got back to ship and found Peregrine White had been born in their absence.
Mon.	4 Dec.	14 "	Dies, Edward Thompson.
Tues.	5 "	15 "	Francis Billington nearly blows up the Mayflower.
Wed.	6 "	16 "	Third exploring party started in the shallop, and get as far as Eastham. Jasper Moore dies on the ship.

Day.	Old Style.	New Style.	1620.
Thurs.	7 *Dec.*	17 *Dec.*	Explored up Welfleet Bay, and inland, and slept at Great Meadow Creek ; Bradford's wife falls overboard from the ship, and is drowned.
Fri.	8 "	18 "	Had first encounter with Indians, then coasted round the bay, following the shore westward and northward, went by Barnstable in a snow storm so thick they did not see its harbor, broke their rudder, split their mast into three pieces, and in a heavy northeaster ran in under the lee of Clark's Island in Plymouth harbor after pitch dark. James Chilton dies on the ship.
Sat.	9 "	19 "	Rested, refitted their mast and rudder, etc.
Sab.	10 "	20 "	*Kept the Sabbath* on Clark's Island.
Mon.	11 "	21 "	FOREFATHERS' DAY. Landed on the Rock, and explored.
Tues.	12 "	22 "	Started back for Provincetown, and the Mayflower.
Fri.	15 "	25 "	Weighed anchor for Plymouth, but a foul wind drove them back.
Sat.	16 "	26 "	Dropped anchor inside Plymouth beach.
Mon.	18 "	28 "	Party from the ship landed and explored.
Tues.	19 "	29 "	Second exploration of the shore.
Wed.	20 "	30 "	Third expedition, resulting in decision to settle near what are now Burial Hill and Town Brook.
Thurs.	21 "	31 "	Stormed, and nothing could be done, but Richard Britteredge dies on the ship.

$162\frac{0}{1}$.

Day.			
Fri.	22 "	1 *Jan.*	Storm continues. Goodwife Allerton gives birth to a still-born son.
Sat.	23 "	2 "	As many as can, begin to cut and carry timber on shore for the common house.
Sab.	24 "	3 "	Those on shore hear a cry of savages — as they think, but see none. Solomon Prower dies.
Mon.	25 "	4 "	Busy on the common house. Indian alarm again, but saw none. The beer being low, they begin to drink water on board the ship.
Tues.	26 "	5 "	Foul weather, no going ashore.
Wed.	27 "	6 "	To work again.
Thurs.	28 "	7 "	Divided whole company into nineteen families, and measured out lots for them.
Fri.	29 "	8 "	Tried to work, but rainy.
Sat.	30 "	9 "	Same weather and same result. Saw Indian smokes in the distance.
Mon.	1 *Jan.*	10 "	At work again. Digory Priest dies.
Wed.	3 "	13 "	More smokes seen, but still no Indians.
Thurs.	4 "	14 "	Standish and a party go out, and find wigwams, but no Indians. Shot an eagle, and the poor hungry men likened its flesh to mutton !

Day.	Old Style.	New Style.	162$\frac{0}{1}$.
Fri.	5 *Jan.*	15 *Jan.*	A sailor found a herring, so they hoped for fish soon, but found they had no hooks small enough for cod-hooks.
Sat.	6 "	16 "	C. Martin very sick, and sends ashore for Governor Carver to see him "about his accounts."
Sab.	7 "	17 "	Carver goes on board.
Mon.	8 "	18 "	Fine, fair day. Shallop gets some fish. F. Billington discovers the pond since called by his name. Martin dies.
Tues.	9 "	19 "	Divided their lots of land by lot, laying out a street with cabins on each side.
Thurs.	11 "	21 "	William Bradford taken sick while at work.
Fri.	12 "	22 "	Rained again. John Goodman and Peter Brown lost themselves in the woods, chasing a deer.
Sat.	13 "	23 "	An armed party went out seven or eight miles in search vainly, but at night, the lost men returned, faint and frozen, so that Goodman's shoes had to be cut from his feet, and it was a long time before he was able to walk.
Sab.	14 "	24 "	More being now on shore than in the ship, they intended to have worship in the common house, but its thatch took fire and burned off, which prevented.
Mon.	15 "	25 "	Stormed again, so that there was no communication between the ship and the shore.
Tues.	16 "	26 "	Three fair, sunshiny days, like April, followed, and cheered on their work.
Fri.	19 "	29 "	Began to build a shed to store their provisions. Stormed again. Saw two wolves.
Sat.	20 "	30 "	Made their shed.
Sab.	21 "	31 "	*Kept their first Sabbath worship ashore.*
Mon.	22 "	1 *Feb.*	Fair. Stored their meal, etc., in the shed.
Mon.	29 "	8 "	Cold with sleet, but cleared, and the long-boat and shallop carried goods ashore. Miles Standish's wife Rose, dies.
Tues.	30 "	9 "	Frosty, with sleet. Could not work.
Wed.	31 "	10 "	More so. Those on the ship saw two Indians running away.
Sab.	4 *Feb.*	14 "	Wet, and so windy as almost to blow the Mayflower (now light), from her anchorage, and the windy flood almost washed the "daubing" out of the chinks of their cabins.
Fri.	9 "	19 "	Too cold to work. The cabin of the sick ones caught fire, but was put out without much damage to them. Killed five geese, and found a dead deer.
Fri.	16 "	26 "	Cold. One fowling saw twelve Indians, and heard more. The said Indians made a great fire at night in the woods, and stole some tools that had been left out.

Day.	Old Style.	New Style.	$162\frac{0}{1}$.
Sat.	17 Feb.	27 Feb.	Began to organize in a military way. Chose Miles Standish Captain. Two savages made signs on a near hill, but ran away.
Wed.	21 "	3 Mar.	Got the great guns out of the ship, and mounted them on what is now Burial Hill. William White, William Mullins, and two others die.
Sab.	25 "	7 "	Isaac Allerton's wife Mary dies.
Sat.	3 Mar.	13 "	The birds sang, and there was a thunder-storm.
Wed.	7 "	17 "	Began to sow garden seeds.
Fri.	16 "	26 "	A second meeting to arrange military affairs was broken up by *Samoset's* coolly walking in upon them "straight to the Randevous," and in tolerable English, making the brief speech of "Welcome Englishmen." He told them that all the Indians about Plymouth had died four years before by an extraordinary plague. They fed him, and lodged (and watched) him over night.
Sat.	17 "	27 "	Dismissed him with presents.
Sab.	18 "	28 "	*Samoset* came back, with five others, "to trade," and bringing the stolen tools. Tried to send them away, because it was Sunday, but *Samoset* pretended to be sick, and wouldn't go.
Mon.	19 "	29 "	Fair. Sowed seeds.
Tues.	20 "	30 "	Ditto.
Wed.	21 "	31 "	Sent *Samoset* off. Another military meeting again interrupted by the sight of Indians on the hill. The carpenter, long sick, got well enough to repair the shallop, so they could "fetch all from aboard" — so they cleaned out the ship, and their colonizing became complete.
Thurs.	22 "	1 Apr.	Another fine day, and another attempt at public business interrupted by the return of *Samoset*, bringing *Squanto*, (the only survivor of the Indians native to the spot,) and announcing *Massasoit*, who, with his brother, *Quadequina*, and suit, made a formal call, and concluded a treaty — which was kept by both parties, until Philip broke it in 1675.
Fri.	23 "	2 "	Visits exchanged between the colonists and *Massasoit's* party. *Squanto* went to fish for eels, which he trod out of the mud with his feet, and caught with his hands, and which the colonists thought "very fat and sweet." Concluded their military and other public business, and re-elected John Carver for Governor, for the new year, beginning on Sabbath the 25th.
Sat.	24 "	3 "	Edward Winslow's wife, Elizabeth, dies. A great mortality prevailed during this month, above the names here given. Nearly half the sailors of the Mayflower died also.

Day.	Old Style.	New Style.	**1621.**

Tues.   5 *Apr.*   15 *Apr.*   The Mayflower starts for England on her return voyage, but none of the diminished company wanted to go back in her.

——   — "   — "   Governor Carver died suddenly, "and his wife being a weak woman, dyed within 5 or 6 weeks after him." William Bradford was chosen Governor in his place, "and being not yet recoverd of his ilnes, in which he had been near ye point of death, Isaak Allerton was chosen to be an Assistante unto him."

Sat.   12 *May.*   22 *May.*   Edward Winslow was married to Mrs. Susanna, widow of William White, who had died, $\frac{21\ \text{Feb.}}{3\ \text{Mar.}}$ The first marriage in the Colony.

Mon.   18 *Jun.*   28 *Jun.*   Two servants fight a duel, each wounding the other. The company sit on their case, and adjudge them to have their head and feet tied together, and so to lie for twenty-four hours without meat or drink ; but "within *an Hour*, because of their great Pains, at their own & their Master's [Stephen Hopkins] humble Request, upon Promise of better Carriage, they are released by the *Governor*."

"The spring now approaching, it pleased God the mortalitie begane to cease amongst them, and ye sick and lame recovered apace, which put, as it were, new life into them ; though they had borne their sadd affliction with as much patience & contentedness, as I thinke any people could doe. But it was ye Lord which upheld them, and had beforehand prepared them ; many having long borne ye yoake, yea, from their youth." — Gov. Bradford's *Hist. Plim. Plant.* 98.

VARIOUS EXTRACTS, ETC.,

RISE, CONDUCT, HISTORY, OPINIONS, TRIALS AND INFLUENCE, OF THE PLYMOUTH MOVEMENT, AND MEN.

From the rise of the Papacy to the Reformation, the theory of the Church was that of an all-embracing centralized organism ; governed by the Papal Hierarchy, and whose private members had simply the right, duty, and responsibility, of submission and unquestioning obedience.

Wycliffe.

"Upwards of a century and a half before the time of Luther, Wycliffe had exposed the superstition and despotism of Rome. Born in the early part of the fourteenth century, [near Richmond, Yorkshire, 1324, died at Lutterworth, 31 Dec. 1384,] he anticipated the discoveries of his more fortunate successors, and labored with an assiduity and rectitude of purpose, which entitle him to the admiration and gratitude of posterity. Though his labors did not effect an alteration in the ecclesiastical polity of his country, they made an extensive and permanent impression. A numerous class of followers were raised up, by the Providence of God : these preserved the precious seed of the kingdom until more propitious days ; and, though assailed by the fiercest persecutions, were enabled to hand down the sacred deposit to the times of the Lutheran reformation." — Price's *History of Prot. Non-Conform.* i : 4.

About 1380, Wycliffe completed a translation of the Bible into English — the first ever made public. "It was not made for his own use, but for the enlightenment of his country. His object was to throw the broad blaze of revelation upon the corruptions of the Church, to expose before his fellow-men the errors and superstitions into which they had fallen, and to disclose to their view the narrow path which they had missed. The numerous copies of Wycliffe's translation preserved for four centuries and a half, attest the early publicity of his version, and the diligent means employed for the multiplication of transcripts. It may safely be affirmed that not one of the partial versions previously made, had ever been as widely diffused as this ; and it was the formation of the bold idea of its general circulation, and the execution of the daring and unexampled project, that constitute the peculiar and glorious characteristic of the reformer's enterprise."— Bagster's *English Hexapla.* 13.

"The disciples of Wycliffe were termed Lollards, and were found in most parts of the kingdom. Knighton, a canon of Leicester, and a cotemporary of Wycliffe, tells us that in the year 1382, 'their number very much increased, and that, starting like saplings from the root of a tree, they were multiplied, and filled every place within the compass of the land.' This language must undoubtedly be understood with some limitation ; but we cannot mistake the inference to be drawn from it." — Vaughan's *Life of Wycliffe.* 154.

" One thing I boldly assert, that in the Primitive Church, or the time of Paul, two orders of the clergy were held sufficient — those of priests and deacons. No less certain am I, that in the time of Paul, presbyters and bishops were the same, as is shown in 1 Tim. iii, and Titus i." — Wycliffe, *Trialogue*, xiii.

" Wycliffe was the first of Puritans, as well as of Protestants." — *Bogue and Bennett*, i : 27.

" Nothing came to the birth in the 16th century, that had not lain in embryo in Wycliffe's time, under the common heart of England." — Palfrey's *Hist. New England*, i : 108.

" Hitherto, the corpse of John Wycliffe had quietly slept in his grave, about one and forty years after his death, till his body was reduced to bones, and his bones almost to dust ; for though the earth in the chancel of Lutterworth in Leicester-shire, where he was interred, hath not so quick a digestion with the earth of Aceldama, to consume flesh in twenty-four hours, yet such the appetite thereof, and all other English graves, as to leave small reversions of a body after so many years. But now, such the spleen of the Council of Constance, as they not only cursed his memory, as dying an obstinate heretic, but ordered that his bones (with this charitable caution, if it may be discerned from the bodies of other faithful people) to be taken out of the ground and thrown far off from any Chris-tian burial. In obedience hereunto, Richard Flemyng, bishop of Lincoln, diocesan of Lutterworth, sent his officers, (vultures with a quick sight-scent at a dead carcass) to ungrave him accordingly. To Lutterworth they came, (sumner, com-missary, official, chancellor, proctors, doctors and the servants, so that the remnant of the body would not hold out a bone amongst so many hands) take what was left out of the grave, and burnt them to ashes, and cast them into Swift, a neighboring brook running hard by. Thus this brook hath conveyed his ashes into Avon, Avon into Severn, Severn into the narrow seas, they into the main ocean ; and thus the ashes of Wycliffe are the emblem of his doctrine, which now is dispersed all the world over." — Fuller's *Church Hist. Brit.* ii : 423. See also Fox's *Martyrology*, i : 606.

> "Thus speaks (that voice which walks upon the wind,
>   Though seldom heard by busy human kind),
> ' As thou these ashes, little brook, wilt bear
> ' Into the Avon, Avon to the tide
> ' Of Severn, Severn to the narrow seas,
> ' Into main ocean they, this deed accurst
> ' An emblem yields to friends and enemies,
> ' How the bold teacher's doctrine, sanctified
> ' By truth, shall spread throughout the world dispersed !' "— *Wordsworth*.

Henry the VIII and the Reformation.

For the reason that the Pope would not divorce him from Katharine, his wife, when he was tired of her and wanted to marry Ann Boleyn, Henry divorced the Church of England from that of Rome, really founding a new Church in England.

"The existence of the Church of England as a distinct body, and her final separation from Rome, may be dated from the period of the divorce."—Short's *Hist. Ch. Eng.*, 102.

"Upwards of five years were employed by Henry in negotiating with the Papal Court. Wearied at length with its procrastination, he ordered Cranmer to pronounce the sentence of divorce. The Archbishop accordingly declared the marriage of the king with the lady Katherine, null and void ; and on his return to Lambeth, he confirmed the marriage of Henry with Ann Boleyn, which had been privately solemnized by Dr. Lee, some months before. This step precipitated the king into a course of measures hostile to the papacy."—Price's *Hist. Prot. Non-Conf.*, i : 22.

"Henry perhaps approached as nearly to the ideal standard of perfect wickedness, as the infirmities of human nature will allow."—Sir. James Mackintosh's *Hist. of Eng.*, ii : 205.

"The doctrine of the regal supremacy in ecclesiastical matters, had been familiar to Englishmen for many generations. It had been successfully maintained up to a certain point, by the greatest of the Plantaganet kings, and had been ably vindicated by Wycliffe, one of whose cardinal heresies consisted in the denial of the supremacy of the Pope. All that Henry did was to apply and extend a doctrine that had long been filtering through the minds, both of the aristocracy and the commonalty. Hence the otherwise inexplicable circumstance, that his assumption of unlimited supremacy excited only what may be described as a professional opposition. . . . . In that age indeed, there seemed to be no alternative between the supremacy of the Pope and the supremacy of the king. The minds of the best of men, as is the case with some even in these days, were so warped by the influence of ancient ecclesiastical precedents, that none dreamed of an ultimate appeal to Holy Scripture. St. Paul, if he were consulted, was to be interpreted by Augustine, St. John by Jerome, and St. Peter by the Popes ; and to the interpreters, as a matter of course, was given the principal authority. A Church of Christ, independent, as such, of human control, and existing apart from State-craft, was an idea almost impossible to that age. If entertained at all, it could only have been by men as humble in life as in spirit, such as afterwards rose to assert the spiritual character of the kingdom of Christ upon earth."—Skeats's *Hist. Free Ch's of Eng.*, 3.

"The king himself undertook to settle what the people should believe, and with this view, drew up a set of articles of religion. . . . . The new articles might have secured a much wider acceptance than it befell them to receive, but for a step altogether fatal to many of their doctrines, and almost equally fatal to the doctrine of the royal supremacy. The king not only authorized a translation of the Bible into English, but ordered a copy of it to be set up in each of the churches. This act, however, was soon felt to be, what it undoubtedly was, a political blunder, and, after seven years, was substantially recalled. Before furnishing his subjects with such a weapon of almighty power against the system which he had determined to establish, the king issued the "Injunctions." He, who was the slave of his own lusts, enjoined the clergy to exhort the people to 'keep God's commandments,' and to give themselves to 'the study of the Scriptures, and a good life.' In the 'Institution of a Christian Man,' the bishops laid down, at greater length, the creed of the Reformed Church, which was further vindicated in the 'Necessary Doctrine.' Having thus explained and apparently demonstrated the absolute truth of the new theological system, it only remained to enforce it. Some denied the corporal presence, and were accordingly sent to Smithfield. In order to strengthen his power, the king allowed his Parliament to assume the functions of a Convocation, and debate for eleven days the doctrines of the Christian religion. This debate issued in the adoption of the law of the 'Six Articles,' which set forth, in the strongest language, the presence of the natural body and blood of Christ in the Sacrament of the Lord's Supper, sanctioned Communion in one kind only, denied the right of marriage to the priesthood, enforced vows of chastity, allowed private masses, and declared auricular confession to be both expedient and necessary. The most fearful penalties were attached to any opposition to these doctrines. The least was the loss of goods; the greatest, burning at the stake—which was the punishment for denying the first of the Articles. The law was now let loose against both Protestants and Catholics, but with peculiar vengeance against the former. . . . . And so the new Church was founded. The work begun by one royal profligate was, a hundred and thirty years later, fittingly finished by another. Henry the VIIIth's natural successor in ecclesiastical politics is Charles the IId."—*Ibid*, 5.

Rise of Puritanism, etc.

John Hooper, Bishop of Gloucester, was the first father of Puritan Non-conformity. "History, while it has done justice to the character and the abilities of this eminent man, has not done similar justice to his opinions. He appears on its pages as a conscientious opponent of all ecclesiastical ceremonies and habits that are not expressly warranted by Scripture, as a sufferer for his opinions on this subject, and as a martyr for the Protestant religion; but he was more than this. All Protestants and Puritans have been accustomed to hold his name in reverence, but it belongs in a more especial manner to the English Non-conformists of the nineteenth century. It was his voice which first publicly proclaimed the principles of religious freedom. He stood alone amongst the English Protestants of his age in denying the right of the State to interfere with religion."—*Ibid*, 8.

"Touching the superior powers of the earth, it is not unknown to all them that hath read and marked the Scripture, that it appertaineth nothing unto their office to make any law to govern the conscience of their subjects in religion. Christ's kingdom is a spiritual one. In this, neither Pope nor king may govern. Christ alone is the governor of His Church, and the only law-giver."—Hooper's *Declaration of X. Com's.*, 280.

"He told the people, in words proclaimed to thousands at Paul's Cross, and throughout various parts of the kingdom, that their consciences were bound only by the Word of God, and that they might with it, judge 'Bishop, Doctor, preacher and curate.'"—Skeats *ut sup*, 9.

"Mr. Foxe [Acta et Mon, 1587,] recordeth how yt besids those worthy martires & confessors which were burned in queene Mary's days & otherwise tormented, *Many (both students and others) fled out of ye land, to ye number of* 800. *And became severall congregations. At Wesell, Frankford, Bassill, Emden, Markpurge, Strausborough, & Geneva, &c.* Amongst whom (but especialy those at Frankford) begane yt bitter warr of contention & persecutn aboute ye ceremonies and servise booke, and other popish and anti-christian stuffe, the plague of

England to this day, which are like yᵉ high-plases in Israell, wᶜʰ the prophets cried out against, & were their ruine ; which yᵉ better parte sought, according to yᵉ puritie of yᵉ gospell, to roote out and utterly to abandon. And the other parte (under veiled pretences) for their ouwn ends & advancements, sought as stifly to continue, maintaine & defend. . . . . . The one side laboured to have yᵉ right worship of God & discipline of Christ established in yᵉ church, according to yᵉ simplicity of yᵉ gospell, without the mixture of mens inventions, and to have & to be ruled by yᵉ laws of Gods Word, dispensed in those offices, & by those officers of Pastors, Teachers, & Elders, &c. according to yᵉ Scripturs. The other partie, though under many colours & pretences, endeavored to have yᵉ episcopall dignitie, (affter yᵉ popish maner) with their large power & jurisdiction still retained ; with all those courts, cannons & ceremonies, togeather with all such livings, revenues & subordinate officers, with other such means as formerly upheld their anti-christian greatnes, and enabled them with lordly & tyranous power to persecute yᵉ poore servants of God." —Gov. Bradford's *Hist. Plim. Plant.*, 3.

[For a very interesting, minute and authentic history of this establishment (per force,) of separate churches on Continental soil, and the difficulties which beset them, some light from which directed later Separatists to a wiser path, see *A Briefe Discourse of the Troubles Begun at Frankeford in Germany, An. Dom. 1554, About The Booke of Common Prayee and Ceremonies, and continued by the English men there, to the end of Q. Maries Raign, etc. etc.* 4to, pp. 184, published in 1575, and reprinted in London in 1642.]

The Puritan Struggle.

"During the forty-four years of the reign of Elizabeth, the whole power of the crown was exercised, in regard to ecclesiastical matters, with two distinct purposes. The first was to subject the Church to its 'governor,' the second to suppress all opinions differing from those which had received a special patent of protection. The first wholly succeeded ; the second wholly failed. The Prayer-book and Articles of Elizabeth do not materially differ from those of Edward. The only difference of any importance relates to the vestments, which were ordered to be the same as those in use in the second year of Edward. This change was against a further reformation, and it was confirmed by a third Act of Uniformity. The Queen soon let it be known that this Act was not to be a dead letter. She heard of some who did not wear the habits, and who even preached against them, and Parker was at once ordered to enforce the law. Then the exiles who had returned from the Continent, flushed with hope, and ardent in the cause of the Gospel, found the paw of the lion's cub as heavy as that of the royal beast himself . . . . So zealously did he [Parker — the Primate,] set about his work that he shocked the statesmen of his age, and at last shocked even Elizabeth herself. Not being an ecclesiastic, there was a limit to the queen's capacity of creating and afterwards enjoying the sight of human suffering. There was no such limit in Parker. The jackall's appetite was, for once, stronger even than that of the lioness. The attempt to enforce the Act of Uniformity excited instant resistance, and the Church was turned into a great shambles." — Skeats *ut sup.* 13.

"There must be a reason, apart from the character of the governing power, why Puritans within the Church have never succeeded. The reason is probably to be found in the fact that they never essentially differed from the dominant party. Both were almost equally intolerant. Parker and Whitgift persecuted the Puritans; but if Cartwright had been in Whitgift's place, he would have dealt out equal persecution to Baptists and Independents. They, who had suffered imprisonment on account of their opinions, actually remonstrated with statesmen for releasing Roman Catholics from confinement. They held a purer doctrine than their opponents held, but none the less did they require it to be enforced by the 'authority of the magistrates.' It seems strange that men who devoted so much time to the study of the Scriptures, and whose knowledge of them was as extensive as it was profound, should have missed the one study, which to a Christian, would seem to be the most obvious, the life and character of the Founder of their religion and the nature of His mission. But, habits of thought are more tyrannical than habits of action; and the habit of theological thought was then, as for generations afterwards, essentially dogmatical. The best of the Puritans looked to the Scriptures for rules rather than for principles, for propositions rather than for examples. Christianity was, with them, merely an historical development of Judaism; and therefore, while they believed in the sacrifice of Christ, they equally believed in the laws of Moses. The Sacred Writings were rough materials, out of which they might hew their own systems. The stones were taken in equal parts out of the books of the Old Testament and the New, the latter being dug for doctrine and the former for precept. Amongst all the works of the early Puritans, there is not one on the character or life of Christ, nor one which gives any indication that they had even an imagination of the wholly spiritual nature of His kingdom. Whatever that kingdom might be in the place Heaven, on the place Earth it was to be fenced and extended by pains and penalties, threatenings and slaughter. They denied the supremacy of the civil magistrate in religion, but it was only in order to assert their own supremacy. They pleaded with tears for liberty of conscience, and would have denied it to the first 'Anabaptist' whom they met. It was no wonder they did not gain their end, and no wonder that they scarcely hoped to gain it. It would seem that the English race required to be transplanted before it could bear a more perfect flower and fruit than any of which Puritanism only was capable. That service was effected by Elizabeth." — *Ibid*, 20.

The Evolution of Independency.

"There were certainly Baptist churches in England as early as the year 1589, and there could scarcely have been several organized communities without the corresponding opinions having been held by individuals, and some churches established for years previous to this date. With respect to the Independents, certain 'congregations' are spoken of by Foxe [Vol. iii: 114,] as established in London in A. D. 1555, and it is possible that they were Independent, but more probable that they were Puritan. It is now clearly established that an Independent church, of which Richard Fitz was pastor, existed in A. D. 1568 [*Congregational Martyrs*, Art. R. Fitz.] In A. D. 1580, Sir Walter Raleigh spoke of the Brownists as existing 'by thousands.' . . . . But although Richard Fitz was the first pastor of the first Independent church in England, to Robert Browne belongs the honor of founding the denomination. This man's character has been assailed with almost equal virulence by Church and Non-conformist writers; but, although he is proved to have been naturally of a passionate, dogmatic and weak nature, no charge against his piety has been successfully established. [See Fletcher's *Hist. Independ.*, ii : chap. 3.] His moral courage and his willingness to bear suffering in testimony of his sincerity, were amply shown by his life. If, like Cartwright, he eventually returned to the Church, he did what ought not to excite surprise. The wonder is, not that human nature was so weak in him, but that it was so strong in others." — *Ibid*, 22.

"The principles which Browne advocated were substantially the same as those which are now held by the majority of English dissenters. He maintained that the Christian Church is a voluntary association of believing men, that it is competent to the management of its own affairs, and is capable of existing under every form of civil government which human society can assume. He consequently repudiated its subjection to the State, and denied the possibility of its sustaining a national character. It necessarily followed from these principles, that he should denounce the hierarchy as an unscriptural institution, adapted rather to advance the designs of its political supporters, than to promote the religious welfare of mankind. He attacked the whole system of the Established Church, denying the validity of its orders, the purity of its rites, the rectitude of its worship, and the soundness of its constitution. He declaimed against it as a spiritual Babylon, loaded with many of the abominations of the popedom, equally haughty in its spirit, though less powerful to accomplish its intolerant designs." — Price's *Hist. Prot. Non-conf.*, i : 315.

The essential features of Browne's teaching were these :

1. The New Testament the source of all light on Church Government.
2. A Church a body self-associated by a "willing covenant."
3. Church Government the Lordship of Christ, whereby His people "obey to His will."
4. Separation from open and willful offenders, a duty.
5. Church officers are pastors, teachers, elders, deacons, etc., "tried to be meet, and thereto duly chosen by the church which calleth them."
6. Ordination is a pronouncing with prayer and thanksgiving, and laying on of hands "by some of the forwardest and wisest," that those receiving it "are called and authorized of God."
7. Church action is by "general inquiry and consent." — Browne's *Life and Manner of all True Christians.* A. D. 1582. 4to, pp. 112.

What this Brownism really was, as refined from the crudities and sharpnesses of Browne himself, may be excellently seen in the *Confession of Faith of Certaine English People, living in the Low Countreyes, exiled,* which was put forth in 1596, by the Church in Amsterdam, of which Henry Ainsworth was Teacher. Two or three of its articles follow :

" This Ministerie is alike given to every Christian congregation, with like and equall power and commission to have and enjoy the same, as God offereth fit men and meanes, the same rules given to all for the election and execution thereof in all places." — *Art. xxii.*

" As every Christian congregation hath power and commandment to elect and ordeine their own Ministerie acording to the rules in God's word prescribed, and whilest they shall faithfully execute their office, to have them in superabundant love for their worke sake, to provide for them, to honour them and reverence them according to the dignitie of the office they execute: so have they also power and commandment, when anie such default, eyther in their lyfe, doctrine or administration breaketh out, as by the rule of the word debarreth them from, or depriveth them of their Ministerie, by due order to depose them from the Ministerie they exercised; yea, if the case so require, and they remayne obstinate and impenitent, orderly to cut them of by excommunication." — *Art. xxiii.*

"Christ hath given this power to receive in, or to cut of, any member, to the whole body together of every Christian congregation, and not to any one member apart, or to more members sequestred from the whole, or to any other Congregation to do it for them: yet so, as ech Congregation ought to vse the best help they can heerunto, and the most meet member they have to pronounce the same in their public assembly." — *Art. xxiiii.*

"Such as yet see not the truth, may notwithstanding heare the publik doctrine and prayers of the church, and with al meeknes are to bee sought by al meanes: yet none who are growne in yeares may bee received into their communion as members, but such as do make confession of their faith, publickly desiring to be received as members, and promising to walke in the obedience of Christ. Neyther any infants, but such as are the seed of the faithfull by one of the parents, or under their education and government. And further not any from one congregation to be received members in another, without bringing certificate of their former estate and present purpose." — *Art. xxxvii.*

That these were Congregationalists, if they were Brownists, will appear from the following:

"And although the particular Congregations be thus distinct and severall bodies, every one as a compact and knit citie in it self, yet are they all to walke by one and the same rule, and by all meanes convenient to have the counsel and help one of another in all needfull affaires of the Church, as members of one body in the common faith, under Christ their onely head." — *Art. xxxviii.*

Rise and Progress of the Mayflower Church.

"Established here [as postmaster at Scrooby, near Bawtry in England] Brewster, now in the vigor of young manhood, soon took a deep interest in those religious questions which were then agitating the realm. With a mind enlarged by study and travel, he made the acquaintance of Smith, Clyfton, Robinson, and other godly ministers in that [Nottinghamshire] and the neighboring counties, who were conscientiously opposed to the Established Church; and when the policy of deprivation, confiscation, fine and imprisonment was fully entered upon by government to enforce conformity, he cast in his lot with them, and welcomed them to his house [a spacious manor-house of the Archbishop of York, leased to Brewster by Samuel Sandys, eldest son of the then Archbishop] as well as his heart, and in its ample spaces offered them that Sabbath liberty of prophesying which the churches no longer afforded. Gathering together the elect and precious few from the country round about who thought as they thought, and believed what they believed, and were willing to dare what they dared to do; he, with Clyfton and Robinson and those others, some time during 1606, formally — to use Bradford's own words — 'joyned themselves (by a covenant of the Lord) into a church estate, in ye fellowship of ye gospell, to walke in all His wayes, made known, or to be made known unto them, according to their best endeavours, whatsoever it should cost them, the Lord assisting them.'" — *Sabbath at Home*, March, 1867.

" But after these things they could not long continue in any peaceable condition, but were hunted & persecuted on every side, so as their former afflictions were but as flea-bitings in comparison of these which now came upon them. For some were taken & clapt up in prison, others had their houses besett & watcht night and day, & hardly escaped their hands; and ye most were faine to flie & leave their howses & habitations, and the means of their livelehood. Yet these & many other sharper things which affterward befell them, were no other then they looked for, and therfore were ye better prepared to bear them by ye assistance of Gods grace & spirite. Yet seeing them selves thus molested, and that ther was no hope of their continuance ther, by a joynte consente they resolved to goe into ye Low-Countries, wher they heard was freedome of Religion for all men; as also how sundrie from London, & other parts of ye land, had been exiled and persecuted for ye same cause, & were gone thither, and lived at Amsterdam, & in other places of ye land. So affter they had continued together aboute a year, and kept their meetings every Saboth in one place or other, exercising the worship of God amongst them selves, notwithstanding all ye dilligence & malice of their adverssaries, they seeing they could no longer continue in yt condition, they resolved to get over into Holland as they could." — Gov. Bradford's *Hist. Plim. Plant.*, 10.

Emigration to Holland.

" Being thus constrained to leave their native soyle and countrie, their lands & livings, and all their freinds and famillier acquaintance, it was much, and thought marvelous by many. But to goe into a countrie they knew not (but by hearsay), wher they must learne a new language, and get their livings they knew not how, it being a dear place, & subjecte to ye misseries of warr, it was by many thought an adventure almost desperate, a case intolerable, & a misserie worse than death. Espetially seeing they were not aquainted with trads nor traffique, (by which yt countrie doth subsiste) but had only been used to a plaine countrie life, & ye inocente trade of husbandrey. But these things did not dismay them (though they did some times trouble them) for their desires were sett on ye wayes of God, & to injoye his ordinances; but they rested on his providence & knew whom they had beleeved. Yet this was not all, for though they could not stay, yet were yey not suffered to goe, but ye ports & havens were shut against them, so as they were faine to seeke secrete means of conveance, & to bribe & fee ye mariners, & give exterordinarie rates for their passages. And yet were they often times betrayed (many of them) and both they & their goods intercepted & surprised, and thereby put to great trouble and charge." — *Ibid* 11.

" To be shorte, after they had been thus turmoyled a good while, and conveyed from one constable to another, they were glad to be ridd of them in ye end upon any termes; for all were wearied & tired with them. Though in ye mean time they (poor soules) indured miserie enough; and thus in ye end necessitie forste a way for them. . . . . . I may not omitte ye fruite that came hearby, for by these so publick troubls, in so many eminente places, their cause became famouss & occasioned many to looke into ye same; and their godly cariage & Christian behaviour was such as left a deep impression in the minds of many. And though some few shrunk at these first conflicts & sharp beginnings, (as it was no marvell,) yet many more came on with fresh courage, & greatly animated others. And in ye end, notwithstanding all these stormes of oppossition, they all gatt over at length, some at one time & some at an other, and some in one place & some in an other, and mette togeather againe according to their desires, with no small rejoycing." — *Ibid,* 15.

"These Provinces [the Low Countries] were of opinion not only that all religions ought to be tolerated, but that all restraint in matters of religion was as detestable as the Inquisition itself; and accordingly they maintained that nobody erred willfully, or could believe against his conscience, that none but God could inspire right notions into the minds of men; that no religion was agreeable to God, but such as proceeded from a willing heart: experience had also taught them that heterodox opinions could not so effectually be rooted out by human power or violence, as by length of time." — Brandt's *Hist. Ref. in Low Count.,* i : 308.

"Calvinism being thus the established religion of Holland, it will still be seen that entire liberty in belief and practice prevailed there; the only difference being that the followers of any peculiar faith, while they would have the most perfect freedom of worship in their own private houses, or buildings provided by themselves, would not be provided with church edifices at the public expense." — *Sabbath at Home,* March, 1867.

"Twelve or fifteen years before the Scrooby men arrived in Amsterdam, a London company had gone over, who had Francis Johnson for their pastor and Henry Ainsworth for their teacher; and also, as early as 1596, had published their 'Confession of Faith.' Four years before them (in 1604) Smyth of Gainsborough, and his company, — with whom it is not improbable that the Scrooby men were loosely affiliated before they had strength enough to form themselves into a separate church nearer home — had made good their retreat over the North Sea, and were also maintaining themselves on the Amstel. It must in sorrow be added, that these two congregations, of Johnson and Ainsworth, and of Smyth, had not found themselves able to live in that perfect peace which should have adorned their profession of the new faith which they had gathered out of the Word. No means which Robinson or Brewster could apply sufficed to heal the breach. Indeed it soon became evident that — would they, or would they not — the mere living in Amsterdam must involve the new comers in the ill-feeling, and the cross speech. So they prudently resolved to remove thence, before a bad matter was made worse. It is on record in Leyden that John Robinson [*Jan Robartsz*] and 'some of the members of the Christian Reformed Religion born in the kingdom of Great Britain, to the number of one hundred persons, or thereabouts, men and women,' petitioned the magistrates of Leyden for leave to come to Leyden 'by the 1st May next,' to have freedom of the city 'in carrying on their trades without being burdensome to any one.' As this petition — itself without date — is indorsed in the margin under date of 12 Feb. 1609, it seems probable that it had been presented but a few days before that time. The magistrates say in this indorsement, 'they refuse no honest persons free ingress to come and have residence in this city, provided that such persons behave themselves, and submit to the laws and ordinances; and therefore the coming of the memorialists will be agreeable and welcome.' It was beyond a doubt in connection with this cordial response to their application, that the Scrooby church, now, in itself and all its appurtenance, ‘to the number of one hundred, or thereabouts,’ removed, about 1 May 1609, to Leyden." — *Ibid.*

The Character of these Men in Leyden.

"I know not but it may be spoken to ye honour of God, & without prejudice to any, that such was ye true pietie, ye humble zeale, & fervent love, of this people (whilst they thus lived together) towards God and his waies, and yr single harted-nes & sinceir affection one towards another, that they came as near ye primative patterne of ye first churches, as any other church of these later times have done, according to their ranke & qualitie. . . . . Because some of their adversaries did, upon ye rumore of their remoovall, cast out slanders against them, as if that State had been wearie of them, & had rather driven them out (as ye heathen historians did faine of Moyses & ye Isralits when they went out of Egipte) then yt it was their oune free choyse & motion, I will therefore mention a particuler or too to shew ye contrary, and ye good acceptation they had in ye place wher they lived. And first, though many of them weer poore, yet there was none so poore, but if they were known to be of ys congregation, the Dutch (either bakers or others) would trust them in any reasonable matter when yey wanted money. Because they had found by experience how carfull they were to keep their word, and saw them so painfull and diligente in their callings ; yea, they would strive to gett their custome, and to imploy them above others, in their worke, for their honestie & diligence. Againe ; ye magistrats of ye citie, aboute ye time of their coming away, or a litle before, in ye publick place of justice, gave this comendable testemonie of them, in ye reproof of the Wallons, who were of ye French Church in yt citie. These English, said they, have lived amongst us now this 12. years, and yet we never had any sute or accusation came against any of them ; but your strifs and quarels are continuall, &c. . . . . Yea when there was speech of their [the Plymouth men's] remoovall into these parts [this was written in New England] sundrie of note & eminencie of yt nation [the Dutch] would have had them come under them, and for yt end made them large ŏffers." — Bradford *ut sup.*, 19.

"I perswade my selfe, never people upon earth lived more lovingly together, and parted more sweetly then wee the church at Leyden did." — Edward Winslow's *Hypocrisie Unmasked*, 88.

"And that which was a crown unto them, they lived together in love and peace all their days, without any considerable differences, or any disturbance that grew thereby, but such as was easily healed in love ; and so they continued until with mutuall consent they removed into New England." — Gov. Bradford's *Dialogue.*

Why they left Leyden.

"Our Reverend pastor Mr. John Robinson of late memory, and our grave Elder Mr. William Brewster, considering amongst many other inconveniences, how hard the Country was where we lived, how many spent their estate in it, and were forced to return for England ; how grievous to live from under the protection of the State of England ; how like wee were to lose our language, and our name of English; how little good wee did, or were like to do to the Dutch in reforming the Sabbath; how unable there to give such education to our children, as wee ourselves had received, &c. They, I say, out of their Christian care of the flock of Christ committed to them conceived, if God would bee pleased to discover some place unto us (though in America) and give us so much favour with the King and State of England, as to have their protection there, where wee might enjoy the like liberty, and where the Lord favouring our endeavours by his blessing, wee might exemplarily shew our tender Country-men by our example (no lesse burthened than our selves) where they might live, and comfortably subsist and enjoy the like liberties with us, being freed from Anti-christian bondage, keep their names and Nation, and not onely bee a meanes to enlarge the Dominions of our State, but the Church of Christ also, if the Lord have a people amongst the natives whither hee should bring us, &c. Hereby in their grave Wisdomes they thought wee might more glorifie God, doe more good to our Countrey, better provide for our posterity, and live to be more refreshed by our labours, than ever wee could doe in Holland where we were.

Now these their private thoughts upon mature deliberation they imparted to the Brethren of the Congregation, which after much private discussion came to publike agitation, till at the length the Lord was solemnly sought in the Congregation by fasting and prayer to direct us, who moving our hearts more and more to the worke, wee sent some of good abilities over into England to see what favour or acceptance such a thing might finde with the King."—Ed. Winslow, *ut sup.*, 88.

"After they had lived in this citie about some 11. or 12. years (which is ye more observable being ye whole time of y^t famose truce between that state and ye Spaniards) and sundrie of them were taken away by death, & many others begane to be well striken in years, the grave mistris Experience having taught them many things, those prudent governours [Robinson and Brewster] with sundrie of ye sagest members begane both deeply to apprehend their present dangers, & wisely to foresee ye future, & thinke of timely remedy. In ye agitation of their thoughts, and much discours of things hear aboute, at length they began to incline to this conclusion, of remoovall to some other place. Not out of any newfangledness, or such like giddie humor, by which men are oftentimes transported to their great hurt & danger, but for sundrie weightie & solid reasons; some of ye cheefe of which I will hear breefly touch. And first, they saw & found by experience the hardnes of ye place & countrie to be such, as few in comparison would come to them, and fewer that would bide it out, and continew with them. For many y^t came to them, and many more y^t desired to be with them, could not endure y^t great labor and hard fare, with other inconveniences which they underwent & were contented with. But though they loved their persons, approved their cause, and honoured their sufferings, yet they left them as it weer weeping, as Orpah did her mother in law Naomie, or as those Romans did Cato in Utica, who desired to be excused & borne with, though they could not all be Catoes. For many, though they desired to injoye ye ordinances of God in their puritie, and ye libertie of the gospell with them, yet, alass, they admitted of bondage, with danger of conscience, rather then to indure these hardships; yea, some preferred & chose ye prisons in England, rather then this libertie in Holland, with these afflictions. But it was thought that if a better and easier place of living could be had, it would draw many & take away these discouragments. Yea, their pastor would often say, that many of those w^o both wrate & preached now against them, if they were in a place wher they might have libertie and live comfortably, they would then practise as they did.

"2ly. They saw that though yᵉ people generally bore all these difficulties very cherfully, & with a resolute courage, being in yᵉ best & strength of their years, yet old age began to steale on many of them, (and their great & continuall labours, with other crosses and sorrows, hastened it before yᵉ time,) so as it was not only probably thought, but apparently seen, that within a few years more they would be in danger to scatter, by necessities pressing them, or sinke under their burdens, or both. And therfore according to yᵉ devine proverb, yᵗ a wise man seeth yᵉ plague when it cometh, & hideth him selfe, [Prov. xxii : 3], so they like skillfull & beaten souldiers were fearfull either to be intrapped or surrounded by their enimies, so as they should neither be able to fight nor flie ; and therfor thought it better to dislodge betimes to some place of better advantage & less danger, if any such could be found.

"Thirdly ; as necessitie was a taskmaster over them, so they were forced to be such, not only to their servants, but in a sorte, to their dearest chilldren ; the which as it did not a little wound yᵉ tender harts of many a loving father & mother, so it produced likwise sundrie sad & sorowful effects. For many of their children, that were of best dispositions and gracious inclinations, haveing lernde to bear yᵉ yoake in their youth, and willing to bear parte of their parents burden, were, often times, so oppressed with their hevie labours, that though their minds were free and willing, yet their bodies bowed under yᵉ weight of yᵉ same, and became decreped in their early youth ; the vigor of nature being consumed in yᵉ very budd, as it were. But that which was more lamentable, and of all sorowes most heavie to be borne, was that many of their children, by these occasions, and yᵉ great licentiousnes of youth in yᵉ countrie, and yᵉ manifold temptations of the place, were drawne away by evill examples into extravagante & dangerous courses, getting yᵉ raines off their neks, & departing from their parents. Some became souldiers, others tooke upon them farr vioages by sea, and other some worse courses, tending to dissolutenes & the danger of their soules, to yᵉ great greefe of their parents and dishonour of God. So that they saw their posteritie would be in danger to degenerate & be corrupted.

"Lastly, (and which was not least) a great hope & inward zeall they had of laying some good foundation, or at least to make some way therunto, for yᵉ propagating & advancing yᵉ gospell of yᵉ kingdom of Christ in those remote parts of yᵉ world ; yea, though they should be but even as stepping-stones unto others for yᵉ performing of so great a work.

"These, & some other like reasons, moved them to undertake this resolution of their removall ; the which they afterward prosecuted with so great difficulties." —
Bradford, ut sup., 22.

How it Looked to Them.

"The place they had thoughts on was some of those vast & unpeopled countries of America, which are frutfull & fitt for habitation, being devoyd of all civill inhabitants, wher ther are only salvage & brutish men, which range up and downe, litle otherwise than yᵉ wild beasts of the same. This proposition being made publike and coming to yᵉ scaning of all, it raised many varieble opinions amongst men, and cauzed many fears & doubts amongst them selves. Some, from their reasons & hops conceived, laboured to stirr up & incourage the rest to

undertake & prosecute ye same; others, againe, out of their fears, objected
against it, & sought to diverte from it, aledging many things, and those neither
unreasonable nor unprobable; as that it was a great designe, and subjecte to
many unconceivable perills & dangers; as, besids the casulties of ye seas (which
none can be freed from) the length of ye vioage was such, as ye weake bodys of
women and other persons worne out with age & traville (as many of them were)
could never be able to endure. And yet if they should, the miseries of ye land
which they should be exposed unto, would be to hard to be borne; and lickly,
some or all of them togeither, to consume & utterly to ruinate them. For ther
they should be liable to famine, and nakednes, & ye wante, in a maner, of all
things. The chang of aire, diate, & drinking of water would infect their bodies
with sore sickneses, and greevous diseases. And also those which should escape
or overcome these difficulties, should yett be in a continuall danger of ye salvage
people, who are cruell, barbarous, & most trecherous, being most furious in their
rage and merciles wher they overcome; not being contente only to kill & take
away life, but delight to tormente men in ye most bloodie maner that may be;
fleaing some alive with ye shells of fishes, cutting of ye members & joynts of
others by peesmeale, and broiling on ye coles, eate ye collops of their flesh in
their sight whilst they live; with other cruelties horrible to be related. And
surely it could not be thought but ye very hearing of these things could not but
move ye very bowels of men to grate within them, and make ye weake to quake
& tremble. It was furder objected, that it would require greater summes of money
to furnish such a vioage, and to fitt them with necessaries, than their consumed
estats would amounte too; and yett they must as well looke to be seconded with
supplies, as presently to be transported. Also many presidents [precedents] of
ill success, & lamentable misseries befalne others in the like designes, were easie
to be found, and not forgotten to be aledged; besids their owne experience, in
their former troubles & hardships in their remoovall into Holand, and how hard
a thing it was for them to live in that strange place, though it was a neighbour
countrie, & a civill and rich comone wealth.

It was answered, that all great & honourable actions are accompanied with
great difficulties, and must be both enterprised and overcome with answerable
courages. It was granted ye dangers were great, but not desperate; the difficulties were many, but not invincible. For though their were many of them likly,
yet they were not cartaine; it might be sundrie of ye things feared might
never befale; others by providente care & ye use of good means, might in a
great measure be prevented; and all of them, through ye help of God, by fortitude and patience, might either be borne, or overcome. True it was, that such
attempts were not to be made and undertaken without good ground & reason;
not rashly or lightly as many have done for curiositie or hope of gaine, &c. But
their condition was not ordinarie; their ends were good & honourable; their
calling lawfull & urgente; and therfore they might expect ye blessing of God
in their proceeding. Yea, though they should loose their lives in this action, yet
mighte they have comforte in the same, and their endeavors would be honourable.
They lived hear [in Leyden] but as men in exile, & in a poore condition; and as
great miseries might possibly befale them in this place, for ye 12. years of truce
were now out, & ther was nothing but beating of drumes, and preparing for
warr, the events wherof are allway uncertaine. Ye Spaniard might prove
as cruell as the salvages of America, and ye famine and pestelence as sore hear
as ther, & their libertie less to looke out for remedie.

After many other perticuler things answered & aledged on both sids, it was fully concluded by ye major parte, to put this designe in execution, and to prosecute it by the best means they could." — *Ibid*, 24.

"My brethren have not the faith of our glorious Lord Jesus Christ in respect of persons. But now, if it so come to passe, (which God forbid) that the most being eyther forestalled by prejudice, or by prosperitie made secure, there be few found (especially men of learning, who will so far stoop as to look upon so despised creatures, and their cause) ; this alone remaineth, that we turn our faces & mouths unto thee (o most powerfull Lord, & gratious father) humbly imploreing help from God towards those, who are by men left desolate. There is with thee no respect of persons, neither are men lesse regarders of thee, if regarders of thee, for the worlds disregarding them. They who truly fear thee, and work righteousnes, although constreyned to live by leav in a forrain land, exiled from countrie, spoyled of goods, destitute of freinds, few in number, and mean in condition, are for all that unto thee (O gratious God) nothing the less acceptable : Thou numbrest all their wandrings, and puttest their tears into thy bottels : Are they not written in thy book ? Towards thee, O Lord, are our eyes ; confirm our hearts, & bend thine ear, and suffer not our feet to slip, or our faces to be ashamed, O thou both just and mercifull God." — John Robinson's *Just and Necessarie Apologie*, 72.

How it was at Last Arranged.

"They found God going along with them, and got Sir Edwin Sands [Sandys] a religious Gentleman then living, to stirre in it, who procured Sir Robert Nawnton then principall Secretary of State to King James of famous memory, to move his Majesty by a private motion to give way to such a people (who could not so comfortably live under the Government of another State) to enjoy their liberty of Conscience under his gracious protection in America, where they would endeavour the advancement of his Majestie's Dominions, and the enlargement of the Gospell by all due meanes. This his Majesty said was a good and honest motion, and asking what profits might arise in the part [*ie.* part of the country] wee intended (for our eye was on the most northern parts of Virginia) 'twas answered, Fishing. To which hee replyed with his ordinary asseveration, *So, God have my Soule, 'tis an honest Trade, 'twas the Apostles owne calling*, &c. But afterwards he told Sir Robert Nawnton (who took all occasions to further it) that we should confer with the Bishops of Canterbury and London, &c. Wherupon wee were advised to persist upon his first approbation, and not to entangle our selves with them, which caused our agents to repair to the Virginia Company, who in their Court demanded our ends of going ; which being related, they said the thing was of God, and granted a large Patent, and one of them lent us 300*l.* gratis for three yeares, which was repaid." — Winslow, *ut sup.*, 89.

Bradford goes more into particulars, showing how one disappointment after another delayed, embarrassed and vexed them : especially how uncertain they were made by the course the king pursued in promising "that he would connive at them, & not molest them, provided they carried them selves peaceably." He says : "This made a dampe in ye business, and caused some distraction, for many were afraid that if they should unsetle them selves, & put of their estates, and goe upon these hopes, it might prove dangerous, and prove but a sandie foundation. Yea, it was thought they might better have presumed hear upon without

makeing any suite at all, then, haveing made it, to be thus rejected. But some of
ye cheefest thought other wise, and yᵗ they might well proceede hereupon, & that
ye kings majestie was willing enough to suffer them without molestation, though
for other reasons he would not confirme it by any publicke acte. And furder-
more, if ther was no securitie in this promise intimated, ther would be no great
certainty in a furder confirmation of ye same ; for if after wards ther should be a
purpose or desire to wrong them, though they had a seale as broad as yᵉ house
flore, it would not serve yᵉ turne ; for ther would be means enew found to recall
or reverse it. Seeing therfore the course was probable, they must rest herein on
God's providence, as they had done in other things." — Bradford, *ut sup.*, 29.

"But at last, after all these things, and their long attendance, they had a
patent granted them, and confirmed under yᵉ Companies seale ; but these devis-
sions and distractions had shaken of many of ther pretended freinds, and disap-
pointed them of much of their hoped for & proffered means. By the advise of
some freinds this pattente was not taken in yᵉ name of any of their owne, but in yᵉ
name of Mr. John Wincob (a religious gentleman then belonging to yᵉ Countess
of Lincoline) who intended to goe with them. But God so disposed as he
never went, nor they ever made use of this patente, which had cost them so much
labour and charge. . . . . . A right emblime, it maybe, of yᵉ uncertaine
things of this world ; yᵗ when men have toyld them selves for them, they vanish
into smoke." — *Ibid*, 40.

The Hard Terms which were the Best They could Get.

The hardship of the terms to which they were reduced, shows at once the
slenderness of their means, and the constancy of their purpose. It was agreed to
create a joint stock company on the following plan and conditions.

1. Colonists 16 yrs. old and upwards, and persons contributing £10. each, to
be owners of one share.

2. Colonists contributing £10. in money or provisions, to be owners of two
shares.

3. The partnership to continue 7 years, to the end of which time all profits
and benefits gotten by trade, traffic, trucking, working, fishing, or any other means,
to remain as common stock.

4. The settlers, having landed, to be divided into parties to be employed in
boat-building, fishing, carpentry, cultivation, and manufactures for the use of the
colony.

5. At the end of 7 years the capital and profits to be divided among the
stockholders in proportion to their respective shares in the investment.

6. Stockholders investing at a later period to have shares in the division
proportioned to the duration of their interest.

7. Colonists to be allowed one share for each domestic dependant accompa-
nying them (wife, child or servant) more than 16 yrs. of age ; two shares for every
such person, if supplied at their expense ; and half a share for every dependant
between 10 yrs. and 16 yrs.

8. Each child going under 10 yrs., to have at the division 50 acres of unma-
nured land.

9. To the estates of persons dying before the expiration of the 7 years, allow-
ances to be made at the division proportioned to the length of their lives in the
colony.

10. Till the division all colonists to be provided with food, clothing, and other necessaries, from the common stock.

Two stipulations supposed by the colonists to have been settled, to the effect that they should have two days in each week for their private use, and that at the division, they should be proprietors of their houses and of the cultivated land appertaining thereto, were ultimately disallowed by the *Merchant Adventurers* [*i. e.*, the London merchants who aided them to the money they required for the expedition] to the great disappointment and discontent of the other party. Cushman, who was much blamed for his facility in yielding these points, insisted that, if he had acted differently, the whole undertaking would have fallen to the ground. — Condensed from Palfrey's *Hist. New Eng.*, i : 153.

The Final Decision.

"Our agents returning. wee furthei sought the Lord by a publique and solemn Fast, for his gracious guidance. And hereupon wee came to this resolution, that it was best for one part of the Church to goe at first, and the other to stay, *viz.* the youngest and strongest part to goe. Secondly, they that went should freely offer themselves. Thirdly, if the major part went, the Pastor to goe with them ; if not, the Elder onely. Fourthly, if the Lord should frowne upon our proceedings, then those that went to returne, and the Brethren that remained still there, to assist and bee helpfull to them, but if God should bee pleased to favour them that went, then they also should endeavour to helpe over such as were poore and ancient, and willing to come ; these things being agreed, the major part stayed, and the Pastor with them for the present, but all intended (except a very few, who had rather wee would have stayed) to follow after. The minor part, with Mr. Brewster their Elder, resolved to enter upon this great work (but take notice the difference of number was not great)." — Ed. Winslow, *ut sup.*, 90.

The Start.

" At length, after much travell and these debats, all things were got ready and provided. A smale ship [the Speedwell, of 60 tons] was bought & fitted in Holand, which was intended as to serve to help to transport them, so to stay in ye cuntrie and atend upon fishing and shuch other affairs as might be for ye good & benefite of ye colonie when they cam ther. Another was hired at London, [the Mayflower] of burden about 9. score ; [*i.e.* about 180 tons] and all other things gott in readines. So being ready to departe, they hed a day of solleme humiliation, their pastor [John Robinson] taking his texte from Ezra viii : 21. *And ther at ye river, by Ahava, I proclaimed a fast, that we might humble ourselves before our God, and seeke of him a right way for us, and for our children, and for all our substance.* Upon which he spente a good parte of ye day very profitably, and suitable to their presente occasion. The rest of the time was spente in powering out prairs to ye Lord with great fervencie, mixed with abundance of tears. And ye time being come that they must departe, they were acompanied with most of their brethren out of ye citie, unto a town sundrie miles of called Delfes-Haven, wher the ship lay ready to receive them. So they lefte yt goodly & pleasante citie, which had been ther resting place near 12. years ; but *they knew they were* PILGRIMES [whence the genesis of this name as applied to them] & looked not much on those things, but lift up their eyes to yᵉ heavens, their dearest cuntrie, and quieted their spirits. When they came to yᵉ place they found yᵉ ship and all things ready ; and shuch of their freinds as could not come with them followed after them, and sundrie also came from Amsterdame to see them shipte and to take their leave of them. That night was spent with litle sleepe by yᵉ most, but with freindly entertainmente & christian discourse and other reall expressions of true christian love. The next day, the wind being faire, they went aborde, and their freinds with them, where truly dolfull was yᵉ sight of that sade and mournfull parting ; to see what sighs and sobbs and praires did sound amongst them, what tears did gush from every eye, & pithy speeches peirst each harte ; that sundry of yᵉ Dutch strangers yᵗ stood on yᵉ key as spectators, could not refraine from tears. Yet comfortable & sweete it was to see shuch lively and true expressions of dear & unfained love. But yᵉ tide (which stays for no man) caling them away yᵗ were thus loath to departe, their Reverᵈ pastor falling downe on his knees, (and they all with him) with watrie cheeks comended them with most fervente praiers to the Lord and his blessing. And then with mutuall imbrases and many tears, they tooke their leaves one of an other ; which proved to be yᵉ last leave to many of them." — Bradford, *ut sup.*, 58.

"And when the Ship was ready to carry us away, the Brethren that stayed having againe solemnly sought the Lord with us, and for us, and we further engaging our selves mutually as before ; they, I say, that stayed at Leyden feasted us that were to goe at our Pastors house being large [being, in fact, their usual place of Sabbath assembling] where wee refreshed our selves after our teares, with singing of Psalmes, making joyfull melody in our hearts, as well as with the voice, there being many of the Congregation very expert in Musick ; and indeed it was the sweetest melody that ever mine eares heard. After this they accompanied us to Delphs Haven, where wee were to imbarque, and there feasted us againe, and after prayer performed by our Pastor, where a flood of teares was poured out, they accompanied us to the Ship, but were not able to speake one to another for the abundance of sorrow to part : but wee onely going aboard (the Ship lying to the Key and ready to set sayle, the winde being faire), wee gave them a volley of small shot, and three peeces of Ordinance, and so lifting up our hands to each other, and our hearts for each other to the Lord our God, we departed, and found his presence with us in the midst of our manifold straits hee carryed us thorow. And if any doubt this relation, the Dutch, as I heare, at Delphs Haven preserve the memory of it to this day, [1646] and will inform them." — Ed. Winslow, *ut sup.*, 90.

The Spirit in which They Started.

"At their parting Mʳ Robinson wrote a letter to yᵉ whole company. . . . as also a breefe leter writ at yᵉ same time to Mʳ Carver, in which yᵉ tender love & godly care of a true pastor appears."

In this letter Robinson laments that he is constrained for a while to be bodily absent from them, "by strong necessitie held backe for yᵉ present," and exhorts them to special repentance in view of the circumstances of difficulty and danger surrounding them, and to provide carefully for peace with all men, and neither to give nor take offence. He suggests that, as many of them are strangers to each other, and to each other's infirmities, there will be special need of watchfulness in the matter of both giving and taking offence ; and that their "intended course of ciuill communitie wil minister continuall occasion of offence and will be as fuell for that fire," except they diligently quench it with brotherly forbearance. This allusion he further explains, as follows : "Whereas you are to become a body politik, vsing amongst your selues ciuill gouenment, and are not furnished with any persons of speciall eminencie aboue the rest, to be chosen by you into office of gouernment ; Let your wisedome and godlinesse appeare, not onely in chusing such persons as do entirely loue, and will diligently promote the common good, but also in yeelding vnto them all due honour and obedience in their lawfull administrations ; not beholding in them the ordinarinesse of their persons, but Gods ordinance for your good ; nor being like vnto the foolish multitude, who more honour the gay coate, then either the vertuous mind of the man, or glorious ordinance of the Lord. But you know better things, and that the image of the Lords power and authoritie which the Magistrate beareth, is honorable, in how meane persons soeuer. And this dutie you both may the more willingly, and oughte the more conscionably to performe, because you are at least for the present to haue onely them for your ordinary gouernours, which your selues shall make choise of for that worke." — *Mourt's Relation*, viii-xi.

"In the next place, for the wholesome counsell Mr. Robinson gave that part of the Church whereof he was Pastor, at their departure from him to begin the great worke of Plantation in New England, amongst other wholesome Instructions and Exhortations, hee used these expressions, or to the same purpose [this, by the way, is the first and only authentic version of this famous address] : We are now ere long to part asunder, and the Lord knoweth whether ever he should live to see our faces again ; but whether the Lord had appointed it or not, he charged us before God and his blessed Angels, to follow him no further than he followed Christ. And if God should reveal anything to us by any other instrument of his, to be as ready to receive it, as ever we were to receive any truth by his Ministery : For he was very confident the Lord had more truth and light yet to breake forth out of his holy Word. He took occasion also miserably to bewaile the state and condition of the Reformed Churches, who were come to a period in Religion, and would goe no further then the instruments of their Reformation : As for example, the Lutherans they could not be drawne to goe beyond what Luther saw ; for whatever part of Gods will he had further imparted and revealed to Calvin, they will die rather then embrace it. And so also, saith he, you see the Calvinists, they stick where he left them : A misery much to bee lamented ; For though they were precious shining lights in their times, yet God had not revealed his whole will to them : And were they now living, saith hee, they would bee as ready and willing to embrace further light, as that they had received. Here also he put us in mind of our Church-Covenant (at least that part of it) whereby wee promise and covenant with God and one with another, to receive whatsoever light or truth shall be made known to us from his written Word : but withall exhorted us to take heed what we received for truth, and well to examine and compare, and weigh it with other Scriptures of truth, before we received it ; For, saith he, *It is not possible the Christian world should come so lately out of such thick Antichristian darknesse, and that full perfection of knowledge should breake forth at once.*

Another thing hee commended to us, was, that wee should use all meanes to avoid and shake off the name of *Brownist*, being a meer nickname and brand to make religion odious, and the professors of it to the Christian world ; and to that end, said hee, I should be glad if some godly minister would goe over with you, or come to you, before my comming ; For, said hee, there will be no difference between the unconformable [Non-conformist] Ministers and you, when they come to the practise of the Ordinances out of the Kingdome : And so advised us by all meanes to endeavour to close with the godly party of the Kingdome of England, and rather to study union then division ; *viz.* how neare we might possibly, without sin close with them, then in the least measure to affect division or separation from them." — Winslow's *Hypocrisie Unmasked,* 97.

The Voyage.

" The Speedwell brought her passengers prosperously to Southampton, where they found the Mayflower, which vessel had come round from London with Cushman and others a week before. . . . . . The vessels put to sea with about a hundred and twenty passengers. . . . . Before they had proceeded far on the voyage, the Speedwell proved so leaky that it was thought prudent to return, and both vessels put in at Dartmouth. Repairs having been made, they sailed a second time. But again, when they were a hundred leagues from land, the master of the smaller vessel represented her as incapable of making the voyage, and they put back to Plymouth. This was afterwards believed to be a pretence of the master, who had been engaged to remain a year with the emigrants, and who had repented of his contract. The next resource was to divide the company, and leave a portion behind, while the rest should pursue their voyage in the larger ship. This arrangement was presently made." — Palfrey's *Hist. New Eng.,* i : 158.

" Those that went bak were for the most parte such as were willing so to doe, either out of some discontente, or feare they conceived of ye ill success of ye vioage, seeing so many croses befale, & the year time so fart spente ; but others in regarde of their owne weaknes, and charge of many yonge children, were thought least usefull, and most unfite to bear ye brunte of this hard adventure ; unto which worke of God, and judgmente of their brethern, they were contented to submite. And thus, like Gedions [Gideon's] armie, this small number was devided, as if ye Lord by this worke of his providence thought these few to many for ye great worke he had to doe." — Bradford, *ut sup.,* 69.

" Little is recorded of the incidents of the voyage. The first part was favorably made. As the wanderers approached the American continent, they encountered storms which their overburdened vessel was scarcely able to sustain. Their destination was to a point near Hudson's River, yet within the territory of the London Company, by which their patent had been granted. This description corresponds to no other country than the sea-coast of the State of New Jersey. At early dawn of the sixty-fourth day of their voyage, they came in sight of the white sand banks of Cape Cod. In pursuance of their original purpose, they veered to the south, but, by the middle of the day, they found themselves ' among perilous shoals and breakers ' which caused them to retrace their course. An opinion afterwards prevailed, on questionable grounds, that they had been purposely led astray by the master of the vessel, induced by a bribe from the Dutch, who were averse to having them near the mouth of the Hudson, which Dutch vessels had begun to visit for trade." — Palfrey, *ut sup.,* 162.

"They put to sea again with a prosperus winde, which continued diverce days togeather, which was some incouragemente unto them ; yet according to ye usuall maner many were afflicted with sea-sicknes. And I may not omite hear a spetiall worke of God's providence. Ther was a proud & very profane yonge man, one of ye sea-men, of a lustie, able body, which made him the more hauty ; he would allway be contemning ye poore people in their sicknes, & cursing them dayly with greevous execrations, and did not let to tell them, that he hoped to help to cast halfe of them over board before they came to their jurneys end, and to make mery with what they had ; and if he were by any gently reproved, he would curse and swear most bitterly. But it pleased God before they came halfe seas over, to smite this yong man with a greeveous disease, of which he dyed in a desperate maner, and so was him selfe ye first yt was throwne overbord. Thus his curses light on his owne head ; and it was an astonishmente to all his fellows, for they noted it to be ye just hand of God upon him.

After they had injoyed faire winds and weather for a season, they were incountred many times with crosse winds, and mette with many feirce stormes, with which ye shipe was shroudly shaken, and her upper works made very leakie ; and one of the maine beames in ye midd ships was bowed & craked, which put them in some fear that ye shipe could not be able to performe ye vioage. So some of ye cheefe of ye company, perceiveing ye mariners to fear ye suffisiencie of ye shipe, as appeared by their mutterings, they entered into serious consulltation with ye mr & other officers of ye ship, to consider in time of ye danger ; and rather to returne then to cast them selves into a desperate & inevitable perill. And truly ther was great distraction & differance of opinion amongst ye mariners them selves ; faine would they doe what could be done for their wages sake, (being now halfe the seas over), and on ye other hand they were loath to hazard their lives too desperatly. But in examening of all opinions, the mr & others affirmed they knew ye ship to be stronge & firme under water ; and for the buckling of ye maine beame, ther was a great iron scrue ye passengers brought out of Holland, which would raise ye beame into his place ; ye which being done, the carpenter & mr affirmed that with a post put under it, set firme in ye lower deck, & otherways bounde, he would make it sufficiente. And as for ye decks & uper workes they would calke them as well as they could, and though with ye workeing of ye ship they would not longe keepe stanch, yet ther would otherwise be no great danger, if they did not overpress her with sails. So they comited them selves to ye will of God, & resolved to proseede. In sundrie of these storms the winds were so feirce, & ye seas so high, as they could not beare a knote of saile, but were forced to hull, [to float or drive on the water, like the hull of a ship without sails. — *Webster*] for diverce days togither. And in one of them, as they thus lay at hull, in a mighty storme, a lustie yonge man (called John Howland) coming upon some occasion above ye grattings [a lattice cover for the hatches of a ship. — *Webster*], was, with a seele [lurch] of ye shipe throwne into ye sea ; but it pleased God yt he caught hould of ye tope-saile halliards which hunge over board, & rane out at length ; yet he held his hould (though he was sundry fadomes under water,) till he was hald up by ye same rope to ye brime of ye water, and then with a boat hooke & other means got into ye shipe againe & his life saved ; and though he was something ill with it, yet he lived many years after, and became a profitable member both in church & comone wealthe. In all this viage ther died but one of ye passengers, which was William Butten, a youth, servant to Samuell Fuller, when they drew near ye coast. But to omite other things (that I may be breefe) after longe beating at sea they fell with that land which is called Cape Cod ; the which being made, & certainly knowne to be it, they were not a litle joyfull. After some deliberation had amongst them selves & with yᵉ mͬ of yᵉ ship, they tacked aboute and resolved to stand for yᵉ southward (yᵉ wind & weather being faire) to finde some place about Hudsons river for their habitation. But after they had sailed yͭ course aboute halfe yͭ day, they fell among deangerous shoulds and roring breakers, and they were so farr intangled ther with as they conceived them selves in great danger ; and yᵉ wind shrinking upon them withall, they resolved to bear up againe for yᵉ Cape, and thought them selves hapy to gett out of those dangers before night overtooke them, as by Gods Providence they did. And yᵉ next day they gott into yᵉ Cape-harbor, wher they ridd in saftie." — Bradford, *ut sup.*, 74.

The Outlook from Cape Cod Harbor.

" But hear I cannot but stay and make a pause, and stand half amased at this poore peoples presente condition ; and so I thinke will the reader too, when he well considers yᵉ same. Being thus passed yᵉ vast ocean, and a sea of troubles before in their preparation (as maybe remembred by yͭ which wente before) they had now no freinds to wellcome them, nor inns to entertaine or refresh their weather-beaten bodys, no houses or much less townes to repaire too, [no settlement of any kind within 500 miles] to seeke for succoure. It is recorded in scripture as a mercie to yᵉ apostle & his shipwraked company, yͭ the barbarians shewed them no smale kindnes in refreshing them, but these savage barbarians, when they mette with them (as after will appeare) were readier to fill their sids full of arrows then otherwise. And for yᵉ season it was winter, and they that know yᵉ winters of yͭ cuntrie know them to be sharp & violent, & subjecte to cruell & feirce stormes deangerous to travill to known places, much more to serch an unknown coast. Besids, what could they see but a hidious & desolate wildernes, full of wild beasts and willd men ? and what multituds ther might be of them they knew not. Neither could they, as it were, goe up to yᵉ tope of Pisgah, to vew from this willderness a more goodly cuntrie to feed their hops ; for which way soever they turnd their eys (save upward to yᵉ heavens) they could have litle solace or content in respecte of any outward objects. For sumer being done, all things stard upon them with a wether-beaten face ; and yᵉ whole countrie, full of woods & thickets, represented a wild & savage heiw. If they looked behind them, ther was yᵉ mighty ocean which they had passed, and was now as a maine barr & goulfe to seperate them from all yᵉ civill parts of yᵉ world. If it be said they had a ship to sucour them, it is trew ; but what heard they daly from yᵉ mͬ & company ? but yͭ with speede they should looke out a place with their shallop, wher they would be at some near distance ; for yᵉ season was shuch as he would not stirr from thence till a safe harbor was discovered by them wher they would be, and he might goe without danger ; and that victells consumed apace, but he must & would keepe sufficient for them selves & their returne. Yea, it was mutered by some, that if they gott not a place in time, they would turne them & their goods ashore & leave them.

Let it also be considered what weake hopes of supply & succoure they left behinde them, yͭ might bear up their minds in this sade condition and trialls they were under ; and they could not but be very smale. It is true, indeed, yᵉ affections & love of their brethren at Leyden was cordiall & entire towards them,

but they had litle power to help them, or them selves; and how ye case stode
betweene them & ye marchants at their coming away, hath allready been declared.
What could now sustaine them but ye spirite of God & his grace? May not &
ought not the children of these fathers rightly say: *Our faithers were English-*
men which came over this great ocean, and were ready to perish in this wildernes;
but they cried unto ye Lord, and he heard their voyce, and looked on their adversitie.
Let them therfore praise ye Lord, because he is good & his mercies endure for ever,
etc." — Bradford, *ut sup.*, 78.

Their Social Compact, and its Relation to Modern Republicanism.

"The day before we came to harbour, obseruing some not well affected to
vnitie and concord, but gaue some appearance of faction, it was thought good
there should be an association and agreement, that we should combine togethcr in
one body, and to submit to such government and governours, as we should by
common consent agree to make and chose." — *Mourt's Relation*, 2.

"I shall a litle returne backe and begine with a combination made by them
before they came ashore, being ye first foundation of their govermente in this
place; occasioned partly by ye discontented & mutinous speeches that some of
the strangers amongst them had let fall from them in ye ship — That when they
came a shore they would use their owne libertie; for none had power to comand
them, the patente they had being for Virginia, and not for New-england, which
belonged to an other Government, with which ye Virginia Company had nothing
to doe. And partly that schuch an acte by them done (this their condition considered) might be as firme as any patent, and in some respects more sure. The
forme was as followeth.

In ye name of God, Amen. We whose names are underwriten, the loyall
subjects of our dread soveraigne Lord, King James, by ye grace of God, of Great
Britaine, Franc, & Ireland, king, defender of ye faith, &c. haveing undertaken for
ye glorie of God, and advancemente of ye Christian faith, and honour of our king
& countrie, a voyage to plant ye first colonie in ye Northerne parts of Virginia,
doe by these presents solemnly & mutualy in ye presence of God, and one of
another, covenant & combine our selves togeather into a civill body politick, for
our better ordering & preservation & furtherance of ye ends aforesaid; and by
vertue hearof to enacte, constitute, and frame such just & equall lawes, ordinances,
acts, constitutions, & offices, from time to time, as shall be thought most meete &
convenient for ye generall good of ye colonie, unto which we promise all due submission and obedience.
In witnes whereof we have hereunder subscribed our names at Cap Codd ye
11. of November, in ye year of ye raigne of our soveraigne Lord, King James, of
England, Franc, & Ireland ye eighteenth, and of Scotland ye fiftie fourth. Ano Dom.
1620. [Signed by 41 males, as first declared in Morton's *New England Memorial*,
1669.] — Bradford, *ut sup.*, 89.

Thrown thus suddenly, by their failure to reach their chartered territory, upon
their own resources, and warned by symptoms of insubordination on board ship
on the part of some who had joined them in England who were not of them in
spirit, of dangers which might increase upon them after they went on shore; the
leading spirits of the enterprise seem to have determined at once to test the
experiment whether that primitive and Divinely revealed yet self-constituted and
essentially democratic government which they had found to work so well in the
church, might not work equally well in the state. "Many philosophers have
since appeared, who have in labored treatises, endeavored to prove the doctrine,

that the rights of man are unalienable, and nations have bled to defend and enforce them ; yet in this dark age, the age of despotism and superstition, when no tongue dared to assert, and no pen to write this bold and novel doctrine — which was then as much at defiance with common opinion as with actual power (of which the monarch was then held to be the sole fountain, and the theory was universal, that all popular rights were granted by the crown) — in this remote wilderness, amongst a small and unknown band of wandering outcasts, the principle that *the will of the majority of the people shall govern* was first conceived, and was first practically exemplified. The Pilgrims, from their notions of primitive Christianity, the force of circumstances, and that pure moral feeling which is the offspring of true religion, discovered a truth in the science of government which had been concealed for ages. On the bleak shore of a barren wilderness, in the midst of desolation, with the blasts of winter howling around them, and surrounded with dangers in their most awful and appalling forms, the Pilgrims of Leyden laid the foundations of American liberty."— Baylies' *Hist. New Plym. Col.* i : 29.

" These were the men who produced a greater revolution in the world than Columbus. He in seeking for India discovered America. They, in pursuit of religious freedom established civil liberty, and meaning only to found a church, gave birth to a nation, and in settling a town commenced an empire."—*Ibid.* i: 4.

" This was the birth of popular constitutional liberty. . . . In the cabin of the Mayflower humanity renewed its rights, and instituted government on the basis of ' equal laws ' for ' the general government.' "— Bancroft, *Hist. U. S.* i : 310.

A Glance at the Sorrows of the New Colony.

" In these hard & difficulte beginnings they found some discontents & murmurings arise amongst some, and mutinous speeches & cariags in other ; but they were soone quelled & overcome by ye wisdome, patience & just & equall carrage of things by ye Govr and better part, wch clave faithfully togeather in ye maine. But that which was most sadd & lamentable was, that in 2. or 3. moneths time halfe of their company dyed, espetialy in Jan: & February, being ye depth of winter, and wanting houses & other comforts ; being infected with ye scurvie & other diseases, which this long vioage & their inaccomodate condition had brought upon them ; so as ther dyed some times 2. or 3. of a day, in ye foresaid time ; that of 100. & odd persons, [there were exactly 102 persons in the Mayflower company] scarce 50. remained. And of these in ye time of most distres, ther was but 6. or 7. sound persons, who, to their great comendations be it spoken, spared no pains, night nor day, but with abundance of toyle and hazard of their oune health, fetched them woode, made them fires, drest them meat, made their beads, washed their lothsome cloaths, cloathed & uncloathed them ; in a word, did all ye homly & necessarie offices for them wch dainty & quesie stomaks cannot endure to hear named ; and all this willingly and cherfully, without any grudging in ye least, shewing herein their true love unto their freinds & bretheren. A rare example & worthy to be remembred. Tow of these 7. were Mr William Brewster, ther reverend elder, & Myles Standish, ther Capten & military comander, unto whom my selfe, & many others were much beholden in our low & sicke condition. And yet the Lord so upheld these persons, as in this generall calamity they were not at all infected either with sicknes, or lamnes. And what I have said of these, I may say of many others who dyed in this generall vissitation, & others yet living, that whilst they had health, yea, or any strength continuing, they were not wanting to any that had need of them. And I doute not but their recompence is with ye Lord." — Bradford, *ut sup.*, 90.

"By that time ther corne was planted, all their victals were spente, and they were only to rest on Gods providence ; at night not many times knowing wher to have a bitt of any thing ye next day. And so, as one well observed, had need to pray that God would give them their dayly brade, above all people in ye world. Yet they bore these wants with great patience & allacritie of spirite, and that for so long a time as for ye most parte of 2. years. . . . They haveing but one boat left and she not over well fitted, they were devided into severall companies, 6. or 7. to a gangg or company, and so wente out with a nett they had bought, to take bass & such like fish, by course, every company knowing their turne. No sooner was ye boate discharged of what she brought, but ye next company tooke her and wente out with her. Neither did they returne till they had caught something, though it were 5. or 6. days before, for they knew ther was nothing at home, and to goe home emptie would be a great discouragemente to ye rest. Yea, they strive who should doe best. If she stayed longe or got litle, then all went to seeking of shel-fish, which at low-water they digged out of ye sands. And this was their living in ye somer time, till God sente ym beter ; & in winter they were helped with ground-nuts and foule. Also in ye somer they gott now & then a dear ; for one or 2. of ye fitest was apoynted to range ye woods for yt end, & what was gott that way was devided amongst them." —Bradford, *ut sup.*, 136.

When the *Anne* arrived, "the best dish they [the colonists] could presente their freinds with was a lobster, or a peece of fish, without bread or anything els but a cupp of fair spring water." — *Ibid*, 146.

Their merchant friends in London "went back on them," and their "loving freind" Thomas Weston, failed them, and each new company arriving but became largely new pensioners upon them — coming so ill supplied. As Bradford says : "As they were now fayled of suply by him [Weston] and others in their greatest neede and wants, which was caused by him and ye rest, who put so great a company of men upon them, as ye former company were, without any food, and came at shuch a time as they must live almost a whole year before any could be raised, excepte they had sente some ; so upon yt pointe they never had any supply of vitales more afterwards (but what the Lord gave them otherwise), for all ye company sent at any time was allways too short for those people yt came with it." — *Ibid*, 116.

"But these troubls prodused a quite contrary effecte then their adversaries hoped for. Which was looked at as a great worke of God, to draw on men by unlickly means." — *Ibid*, 189.

"Brewster, the ruling Elder, lived for many months together without bread, and frequently on fish alone. With nothing but oysters and clams before him, he, with his family, would give thanks that they could 'suck of the abundance of the seas, and of the treasures hid in the sands.' Whenever a deer was taken, it was divided amongst the whole company. It is said that they were once reduced to a pint of corn, which being equally divided, gave to each a proportion of five kernels, which was parched and eaten." — Baylies's *Hist. New Plym.*, i : 121.

Reason why They Succeeded where Others had Failed.

"No trading adventurers were so capable and resolute as to be able to plant that soil. . . . . . A religious impulse accomplished what commercial enterprise, commanding money and court favor, had attempted without success. Civilized New England is the child of English Puritanism."—Palfrey, *ut sup.*, i : 101.

"Several attempts were made to plant New England from worldly motives, but they all proved abortive."—Backus's *Hist. New Eng.*, i : 33.

"And now compare this company with that of Sagadahock [Popham's colony, which landed on the Kennebec, 8 Aug., 1607.] That company, who came upon worldly designs, had an hundred men ; this religious society consisted of but one hundred and one souls, men, women and children ; the one arrived at the place designed for settlement in August, the other not till winter had set in. The worldly company only buried their President [Popham], and all returned the next year to their native country again ; whereas this religious people, in about five months' time, buried their Governor and full half their number, and yet with fortitude and patience they kept their station ; yea, though they were afterwards deserted and abused by some who had engaged to help them. We cannot now form an idea of what those pious planters endured to prepare the way for what we at this day enjoy." — *Ibid* i : 40.

"Whether Britain would have had any colonies in America at this day, if religion had not been the grand inducement, is doubtful." — Hutchinson's *Hist. Mass.*, i : 3.

"The question may very naturally be asked, how it happened that a population of adventurers without military force, and with little wealth, which is unquestionably a formidable element of power, and by which men often make their will acceptable ; and with an equality as general as was possible in any country which had a government, could without the sanction of a royal charter, and without the interference of the metropolis, which in infant colonies is generally imperative and absolute, sustain themselves so long without tumults and commotions, and do everything essential to the well-being of the community ? This question finds its solution in the religious character of the people. Worldly objects were with them secondary, and that curse of all small and independent communities, political ambition, found no place amongst them. The higher offices were not sought, but the services of such as were fit to sustain them were demanded as the right of the people, and they were accepted not for the sake of distinction, emolument or pleasure, but from a sense of duty ; fearful of the loss of reputation, men underwent the severe and painful duties which such offices required." — Baylies's *Hist. New Plym.*, iv : 146.

Recognition of their Sufferings and Heroism at the Time.

"If ye land afford you bread, and ye sea yeeld you fish, rest you a while contented, God will one day afford you better fare. And all men shall know you are neither fugetives nor discontents. But can, if God so order it, take ye worst to your selves, with content, & leave ye best to your neighbors, with cherfullnes. Let it not be greevous unto you yt you have been instruments to brake ye ise for others who come after with less dificulty, the honour shall be yours to ye worlds end. We bear you always in our brests, and our harty affection is towards you all, as are ye harts of hundreds more which never saw your faces, who doubtles pray for your saftie as their owne, as we our selves both doe & ever shall, that ye same God which hath so marvelously preserved you from seas, foes, and famine, will still preserve you from all future dangers, and make you honourable amongst men, and glorious in blise at ye last day." — Letter from some of the English adventurers, 1623, copied by Bradford, *ut sup.*, 144.

The following extract from a letter of Gov. Bradford to his wife's sister, Mary Carpenter, still in England, of date $\frac{19}{2}$Aug. 1646, will show the feeling on this subject which prevailed, when the Colony had more than attained its majority :

" We understand, by your letter, that God hath taken to himself our aged mother, out of the troubles of this tumultuous world, and that you are in a solitary condition, as we easily apprehend. We thought good, therefore, to write these few lines unto you, that if you think good to come over to us, you shall be wellcome, and we shall be as helpfull unto you as we may, though we are growne old, and the countrie here more unsettled, than ever, by reason of the great changes that have been in these late times, and what will further be, the Lord only knows, which makes many thinke of removing their habitations, and sundrie of our ministers (hearing of the peace and liberty now in England and Ireland) begin to leave us, and it is feared many more will follow. We do not write these things to discourage you, (for we shall be glad to see you, if God so dispose) but if you find not all things here according to your expectation, when God shall bring you hither, that you may not thinke we dealt not plainly with you."

The Superior Tolerance of the Plymouth Men.

" The spirit of Robinson appeared to watch over his feeble flock on the coast of New England, long after his body was moldering beneath the Cathedral church at Leyden. Again, their twelve years' residence in Holland had brought the Pilgrims in contact with other sects of Christians, and given them a more catholic spirit than pertained to those whose stay in England had been embittered by the strife of contending factions in the Established Church. Whether these reasons fully account for the superior liberality of the Plymouth Colonists, or not, the records show, that as they were distinct from the Puritans in England, and had been long separated from them in Holland, so did they preserve that distinction in some measure in America. The Pilgrims of Plymouth were more liberal in feeling, and more tolerant in practice, than the Puritans of Massachusetts Bay. The simple forms of democratic government [*i.e.*, in its absolute form, precisely as practiced in the Congregational churches] were maintained in Plymouth for eighteen years, until the growth of the Colony compelled the introduction of the representative system." — Arnold's *Hist. Rhode Island*, i : 13.

" The Plymouth Colony was more liberal in its feeling than that of the Bay, permitting a greater latitude of individual opinion." — *Ibid*, 166.

" I have shown that the Pilgrim Fathers, and their precursors, in England, Holland, and at Plymouth, were *Separatists*, and had no connection with the *Puritans*, who subsequently settled in New England, at Salem and Boston, in Massachusetts ; that the principles and practices of the two parties, confounded by some careless writers, differed essentially ; the Separatists ever contending for freedom of conscience and separation from the powers of the State, while the Puritans remained in connection and communion with the State Church, and held, both in England and New England, that the State should be authoritative in matters of religion. Hence the anti-christian and intolerant acts of the Puritan colony [Mass.] to the Separatists — Ralph Smyth, Roger Williams, Isaac Robinson, John Cudworth and Timothy Hatherley. Hence, also, on the arrival of the Friends, the cruel laws for whipping, banishing and executing, for matters of religious faith and practice. I have shown that the Separatist colony of Plymouth had no share in this intolerant conduct during the lives of the Pilgrim Fathers, and, moreover, that they acted kindly, and received into their church both Smyth and Roger Williams when forbidden to worship freely elsewhere ; and that after the death of the Pilgrim Fathers, some of their sons and successors, acting up to their principles, shielded the Friends, and refused to be parties to the persecuting laws then enacted.   .   .   .   .   .   .

It may interest you to know that two eminent historians recently deceased virtually admitted the truth of that which I have thus affirmed. I refer to Lord Macaulay and Earl Stanhope (Lord Mahon), who as Commissioners for decorating, historically, the House of Lords, were appealed to respecting an erroneous inscription placed under Mr. Cope's painting of "The Pilgrim Fathers Landing in New England." The inscription stood : "Landing of a *Puritan* Family in New England," but after listening to the proofs submitted, and hearing Mr. Cope, who stated that he had taken his ideas from Bradford's Journal, the Commissioners ordered the terms "Puritan Family" to be removed, as unjust to the memory of the parties concerned, and substituted the words : 'PILGRIM FATHERS.'"— Mr. Chamberlain Benj. Scott's *The Pilgrim Fathers Neither Puritans Nor Persecutors*, 36.

" Here we may observe the great difference between our Plymouth fathers, and the Massachusetts. With all these stimulations to severity, the Court of Plymouth only charged them [the Seekonk Baptists], to desist from their practice, which others had taken such offence at, and one of them yielding thereto, the others were not so much as bound to their good behaviour, nor any other sureties required."— Backus's *Hist. New Eng.*, i : 214.

" Rigidness is a word that both Episcopalians and Presbyterians have often cast upon our Plymouth fathers. Yet the Massachusetts now discovered so much more of that temper than they, that Mr. Dunstar, in October 24, 1654, resigned his office among them and removed and spent his remaining days at Scituate in Plymouth Colony." — *Ibid*, 284.

" The Plymouth colonists of humbler rank and less excited from having been so long removed from the scene of controversy in England, were more tolerant and mild, and although much swayed by the influence of their domineering neighbors, to whom, on all great occasions, they seemed to defer, were never led into those horrible excesses of fanaticism which disgrace the early annals of Massachusetts."— Baylies's *Hist. New Plym.*, i : 203.

" More fortunate than Massachusetts, they had been undisturbed with sectarian disputes, and wiser, they exercised a liberal toleration, which increased their numbers, while the sterner temper of their neighbors could only be soothed by the banishment of their antagonists." — *Ibid*, i : 321.

" Sectarians, it is true, disturbed the tranquility of the inhabitants of this little Commonwealth ; but persecution with them assumed its mildest form, and

their annals have escaped that deep and indelible stain of blood, which pollutes
the pages of the early history of their sterner and more intolerant brethren of
Massachusetts." — *Ibid*, i : 5.

" Here may be observed to the honor of this Colony, that though the provo-
cations of the Quakers were equally great here as elsewhere, yet they never made
any sanguinary or capital laws against that sect, as some of the Colonies did." —
Appendix to Mr. Robbins' Sermon at Plymouth, (A. D. 1760), p. 15.

Relation of the Plymouth Colony to this Republic.

" The Pilgrims brought with them to the new World a form of Christianity,
which I cannot better describe than by styling it a democratic and republican
religion. This contributed powerfully to the establishment of a republic and a
democracy in public affairs." — *De Tocqueville*, i : 384.

"The system of town governments does not prevail in England. Nothing
analogous to it is known in the Southern States, and although the system of inter-
nal government in the Middle States bears a partial resemblance to that of New
England, it is in many respects dissimilar. Those who are strangers to our
customs are surprised to find the whole of New England divided into a vast
number of little democratic republics, which have full power to do all those
things which most essentially concern the comforts, happiness, and morals of the
people. . . . . Under the government of these little republics,
society is trained in habits of order, and the whole people acquire a practical
knowledge of legislation within their own sphere. To this mode of government
may be attributed that sober and reflecting character, almost peculiar to the
people of New England, and their general knowledge of politics and legislation.
. . . . Now, to the Independent churches we may trace the original notion
of independent communities, which afterwards assumed the name of towns, and
which after having passed through an ecclesiastical state, and after the pro-
prietaries became extinct from the special appropriation of all the lands within
the bounds of their charter, assumed the shape of political corporations with
municipal, and in fact legislative powers within their own limits." — Baylies's
Hist. New Plym., i : 240.

" The purely democratic form of government in the church at Leyden, already
entrenched in the warm affections of the Pilgrims, led to the adoption of a corresponding form of civil government on board the Mayflower for the Colony at
Plymouth. It has been said, and it is true, that it was a Congregational church-
meeting that first suggested the idea of a New England town-meeting ; and a
New England town-meeting embodies all the germinal principles of our State
and national government." — Wellman's *Ch. Pol. of the Pilgrims*, 68.

" The late Dr. Fishback, of Lexington, Ky., a few years since, made the
following statement, which he received from the late Rev. Andrew Tribble, who
died at the age of about 93 years. Mr. Tribble was pastor of a small Baptist
church near Mr. Jefferson's residence, in the State of Virginia, eight or ten years
before the American Revolution. Mr. Jefferson attended the meetings of the
church for several months in succession, and after one of them, asked the worthy
pastor to go home and dine with him, with which request he complied. Mr.
Tribble asked Mr. Jefferson how he was pleased with their [purely democratic,
or Congregational] church government ? Mr. Jefferson replied, that its pro-

priety had struck him with great force, and had greatly interested him ; adding that he considered it the only form of pure democracy which then existed in the world, *and had concluded that it would be the best plan of government for the American Colonies.*" — Belcher's *Relig. Denominations in U. S.*, 184.

"Congregationalism was, historically, the mother of our civil liberties. It was so first at Plymouth, and in the Massachusetts Colony. It was so, later, in the days of the Revolution. And it would seem a natural inference that the same polity which gave us a Republic, would be most favorable, in all its workings, to the permanent welfare of the State." — Dexter's *Congregationalism, etc.*, 290.

"The Plymouth Colony has furnished her full proportion of talent, genius, learning and enterprise in almost every department of life; and, in other lands, the merits of the posterity of the Pilgrims have been acknowledged. . . . . . In one respect they present a remarkable exception to the rest of America. They are the purest English race in the world ; there is scarcely any intermixture even with the Scotch or Irish, and none with the aboriginals. Almost all the present population are descended from the original English settlers. . . . . . The fishermen and navigators of Maine, the children of Plymouth, still continue the industrious and bold pursuits of their forefathers. In that fine country, beginning at Utica (N. Y.) and stretching to Lake Erie, this race may be found on every hill and in every valley ; on the rivers and on the lakes. . . . . . And in all the Southern and South-western States, the natives of the 'Old Colony,' like the Armenians of Asia, may be found in every place where commerce and traffic offer any lure to enterprise ; and in the heart of the gigantic [West], like their ancestors, they have commenced the cultivation of the wilderness, like them, surrounded with savage beasts and savage men, and like them, patient in suffering, despising danger, and animated with hope." — Baylies's *Hist. New Plym.*, iv : 148.

The May-flower on New England's coast has furled her tattered sail,
And through her chafed and moaning shrouds December's breezes wail;
Yet on that icy deck, behold a meek but dauntless band,
Who, for the right to worship God, have left their native land ;
And to this dreary wilderness this glorious boon they bring —
 A Church without a Bishop, and a State without a King !

Those daring men, those gentle wives, say, wherefore do they come?
Why rend they all the tender ties of kindred and of home?
'Tis *Heaven* assigns their noble work, man's spirit to unbind;
They come not for themselves alone — they come for all mankind;
And to the empire of the West this glorious boon they bring —
 A Church without a Bishop, and a State without a King !

Then Prince and Prelate, hope no more to bend them to your sway —
Devotion's fire inflames their breasts, while freedom points their way;
And in their brave heart's estimate, 't were better not to be,
Than quail beneath a despot, where the soul cannot be free :
And therefore o'er a wintry wave, those exiles come to bring
 A Church without a Bishop, and a State without a King !

And still their spirit, in their sons, with freedom walks abroad;
The BIBLE is our only creed, our only sovereign, GOD !
The hand is raised, the word is spoke, the joyful pledge is given —
And boldly on our banner floats, in the free air of Heaven,
The motto of our sainted sires; and loud we'll make it ring —
 A CHURCH WITHOUT A BISHOP, AND A STATE WITHOUT A KING !
       —*Rev. Charles Hall, D.D.*

O little fleet! that on thy quest divine
Sailedst from Palos one bright autumn morn,
Say, has old Ocean's bosom ever borne
A freight of Faith and Hope, to match with thine?

Say, too, has Heaven's high favor given again
Such consummation of desire, as shone
About Columbus, when he rested on
The new-found world, and married it to Spain?

Answer — Thou refuge of the Freeman's need,
THOU for whose destinies no Kings looked out,
Nor Sages to resolve some mighty doubt,
Thou simple MAYFLOWER of the salt-sea mead!

When THOU wert wafted to that distant shore, —
Gay flowers, bright birds, rich odors, met thee not,
Stern nature hailed thee to a sterner lot, —
God gave free earth and air, and gave no more.

Thus to men cast in that heroic mold
Came Empire, such as Spaniard never knew —
Such Empire, as beseems the just and true;
And, at the last, almost unsought, came Gold.

But HE, who rules both calm and stormy days,
Can guard that people's heart, that nation's health
Safe on the perilous hights of power and wealth,
As in the straitness of the ancient ways.
—*Richard Monckton Milnes, (Lord Houghton.)*

Tantae Molis Erat Nov-Anglam Condere Gentem!

www.ingramcontent.com/pod-product-compliance
Lightning Source LLC
Chambersburg PA
CBHW021451090426
42739CB00009B/1709